Advance Praise for
Passed Over and Pissed Off

D1612860

In this important book, Dr. Mia Mulrennan tells the story of the "caught in the middle generation"—of Gen X 30- and 40-somethings squeezed between the huge Boomer and Millennial generations, who have too often been told to "wait their turn", only to be passed over for opportunities in the workforce. It is *way past time* to open the doors wide to Gen X in top leadership positions; they have much to contribute, and as a nation and as a global economy, we need their savvy, their experience, and their diverse skillsets. Thank you, Dr. Mulrennan, for this timely book!

Debby Magnuson, VP of Talent Management, Career Partners International
co-author of *Work With Me: A New Lens on Leading the Multigenerational Workforce*

Dr. Mia Mulrennan is a passionate expert, educator, and speaker in her field. This book is a must read and you will be very excited to learn about the talents of Generation X and what they will bring to your teams.

Pam Borton, Pam Borton Partners, CEO
ICF Senior Executive & Global Leadership Coach

As a Gen Xer myself, I have never found a book that accurately explained who we were as a generation and how we fit in to the bigger corporate picture. Mia has finally created a manual for employers on how to work with and motivate the middle generation of workers that are finally coming into their prime. Her writing is on target in describing our experiences and motivations. I can't wait to hand this book out to my clients!

Wendy Benning Swanson, VERUM Staffing Truth in Recruiting

As one of the most influential and impactful members of my faculty at Georgetown University, Dr. Mulrennan's pivotal work brings new light onto a generation of consumers and employees that have been overlooked in lieu of the general obsession with Millennials. Undoubtedly, her keen assessment of psychology, human capital management, and consumer insights is a must read for employers and brand strategists in every industry.

Gray Shealy, M.Arch., CHE, Executive Director, Master's of Hospitality Management Program, Georgetown University School of Continuing Studies

Dr. Mia Mulrennan is the real deal. This is the story she lived herself and the story of so many Gen X leaders. She writes like she talks … in an intelligent, approachable and thoroughly likable way. If you are looking for solutions that embody leadership without ego, this book is a must-read.

Scott Weiler, Vice President, Marketing & Communications Sonesta Hotels and Resorts

Simply put, Dr. Mulrennan nailed it. She was able to succinctly and eloquently state what I've thought throughout most of my career. As a member of Generation X, I patiently waited for the advancement I believed I earned and deserved, while those younger and less experienced than me moved onward and upward. This is exactly why I started my own company: to empower myself to do more. As a small business owner, I just wish I'd made the leap sooner. Thanks again, Dr. Mulrennan!

Sean Williams, Owner of Williams Software Consulting, LLC

Finally – a book that focuses on Generation X leaders. This book expertly outlines why they should no longer be overlooked. An absolute winner!

Patrick O'Halloran, Board Member, DataLink and Outsell Founder, CEO and Chairman, Entiera

Passed Over and Pissed Off is a must read for <u>all</u> leaders. It is not just a rallying cry for Gen X, but a wake-up call for all of corporate America. It will inspire you to get everyone in your organization working well together. If you are looking for an empowering book to be able to win the talent war, this is it!

Deb Jones, Executive Coach, Speaker, Consultant
JTA Consulting Group

For those of us who already know Mia - and her work in leadership and psychology - we know she is a gifted and remarkable person with a focused commitment to success. For me, two words come to mind: "Noble" and "Warrior." And as an author, she is also both. She provides solutions for gaining better relationships and collaborative outcomes across generations. She is also an effective advocate, telling engaging stories of resilience, perseverance and determination while having lived a story like it of her very own. You will regard this book as a personal gift that will leave you looking for more.

Diane Slevin-Boyle, Technology Sales Leader
Carousel Industries

Dr. Mia Mulrennan has been known as a thought leader, a thoughtful speaker, and the "thinking leader's coach." This book continues that trend. It will really make you think about Generation X; their context *and* their talents.

Scott Peterson, MBA
Payments and Strategy Consultant and Educator

Passed Over and Pissed Off

The Overlooked Leadership Talents of Generation X

ISBN: 978-0-9965450-0-6

Passed Over and Pissed Off

The Overlooked Leadership Talents of Generation X

Mia Mulrennan, Psy.D.

with

Terri Bly

Dedication

This book is dedicated to all of the Gen X leaders out there who "held on" in corporate America and ended up passed over and pissed off. This one's for you.

Contents

Acknowledgments

It takes a village to write a book, and there are so many who have helped make this book possible. Big thanks go to Terri Bly, who "prettied up" and outlined my writing and successfully found in-depth information and articles about Generation X, which is a tall order. She even found photographs online simply from my describing them to her from my memories from childhood. You can find any proverbial needle in a haystack, and I am grateful.

There are many others who helped with this book, and I had a fantastic team who taught me so much and helped me feel confident as a first-time author. Thank you very much Erik Olsrud, Jody Amato, "Eagle Eye" Shelley Gillespie and especially Deborah Louise Brown.

And the biggest thank you of all goes to my incredible family. It takes a family to write an entire life's story, and you have been the very best part of mine. Thank you for putting up with my endless hours of typing and work on many projects (this book being only one of them). I am especially grateful to my husband, Dan, for supporting what I do and keeping all of my dreams alive and well.

The Breakfast Club, 1985[1]

Introduction

Generation X: Who Are They?

Born between 1965 and 1981, the cohort known as Generation X came into adulthood during the 1980s and early 1990s, a period of enormous change. Technology was about to transform the world in ways no one could have anticipated, our country experienced monumental shifts in social and family structures, and both corporate America and the definition of "work" changed in ways no one could have previously imagined.

Pop culture is a perfect reference point to provide some context for Gen X. The list of celebrity Gen Xers includes Gwyneth Paltrow, Angelina Jolie, Robert Downey Jr., Julia Roberts, Matt Damon, Jake Gyllenhal, and Adam Sandler. Some of the well-known business leaders born into this generation include Google founders Larry Page and Sergey

Brin; Yahoo CEO Marissa Mayer; Blake Mycoskie, founder of TOMS Shoes; and Facebook COO and *Lean In* author Sheryl Sandberg.

No longer "kids," Gen Xers have entered that awkward mid-ground between sexy, youthful exuberance, and the graceful, wise, and distinguished aura attributed to middle age. As of the writing of this book (2015), the average age of the entire cast of the movie *The Breakfast Club* is fifty-two. The average age of the entire cast of the television show *Friends*—arguably the poster children of Generation X—is forty-eight. Rob Lowe and Kiefer Sutherland are both over fifty. In short, Gen Xers are the oft-neglected middle children between two noisy, much larger generations.

Besides their age, how are Generation Xers meaningfully different from their older and younger colleagues? As any statistician would be happy to tell you, no matter what you're trying to compare, there will always be more similarities than differences between and within groups of people, and generations are certainly no exception.

Nonetheless, aspects of the culture, people, and events experienced by a group of people at formative moments in their lives impact their attitudes and beliefs. This is the entire premise of social psychology, after all. We talk about the influence of the Great Depression and World War II on "The

Greatest Generation," and the Vietnam War, "hippie" culture, and the civil rights movement shaped much of what we have seen from the Baby Boomers. Already you can find countless articles, books, and workshops discussing the attitudes and beliefs of Millennials, and how their lifelong interaction with technology and ties to their parents have necessitated some serious tweaks to American corporate culture and how we define leadership.

But what about the members of Generation X? Who are *they?* What cultural phenomena, trends, and events have shaped their views and expectations for their lives—and more specifically, for their careers? While top-notch research on the topic is sparse, this book includes information from a number of sources: articles, surveys, interviews, observations from peers in human resources and related fields, as well as my own observations from more than twenty years as a consultant, coach, and industrial/organizational psychologist. I am also a bona fide member of Generation X, born in 1966—the same year as Patrick Dempsey, Salma Hayek, and John Cusack.

One important side note: many in the business world often go too far in making sweeping claims about generations and how they differ, relying on little more than stereotypes and their own perceptions. I hope to avoid painting fifty-one million people—regardless of socioeconomic status, race, or ethnicity—with the same brush. Rather, the goal is to ignite and facilitate a productive conversation and, ideally, even more productive actions among business executives, hiring managers, and Gen X employees at all levels of corporate America.

Part I—Growing Up Gen X

"We're all pretty bizarre. Some of us are just better at hiding it, that's all."

~ Andrew Clark, *The Breakfast Club* (1985)

MISCELLANY / LADY, IS THIS YOUR LITTER?

Lady, is this your litter? 1969. *The Tampa Bay Times*[2]

Chapter 1

With or Without You: an Era of Hands-Off Parenting

Generation X went through its all-important formative years as one of the least-parented, least-nurtured generations in US history.[3]

~ from a study conducted by Reach Advisors

It would be an understatement to say that Generation X children were not parented in the same way that children are raised today. Generation X grew up in a time in America when the family unit was changing and women were going through the second feminist movement. Unlike today, little focus was placed on actively becoming the perfect parent or comparing parenting techniques. Walk through your local bookstore today and the parenting section is immense, with new books coming out all the time. During the 60s and 70s, the foremost expert in childrearing was Dr. Spock, who published his still-popular book on baby and child care in 1946. It was perfectly acceptable as a parent during the 60s and 70s—in fact, even considered cool and "far out"—to focus on your own personal goals.

Among the most important tasks of a typical adult during the 60s were a focus on things like "self-actualization" and "free love." Hence the Baby Boomers were dubbed the "Me Generation."

Look at the photo at the beginning of this chapter. Can you imagine if this photo were taken today? This photo from *LIFE* magazine was considered at the time to be funny and witty. If posted today, the photo would be popular, to be sure, but instead of making its way into the pages of *LIFE*, the more likely outcome would be a mother in jail and a child in foster care faster than you can say "viral."

Notice how the child is jokingly called "litter." We even later called *ourselves* garbage without a thought, and traded "Garbage Pail Kids" cards, something akin to baseball and Pokémon cards. There was even a show on television called *Those Pesky Kids*. Children were simply not seen in the same light as they are today.

The Generation X children were not, on the whole, an overly doted-on bunch. The term "helicopter parent" had not been coined yet! Considered by some as the "anti-child" chapter in American history, the 70s and 80s represented an era in which being a wife and mother was no longer the default number-one priority for many middle-class women. Little cultural focus was placed on what it meant to be the "perfect parent;" mothers rarely sat around comparing parenting techniques, debating over which one was most likely to get their child into an Ivy League school eighteen years down the road. If Baby Boomers were raised by mothers who were told to aspire to get their whites whiter along with June Cleaver, Gen Xers were raised by mothers told to burn their bras along with Gloria Steinem. Women were told that they needed a man like a fish needed a bicycle; babies and children weren't mentioned at all.

With a wider range of available career options, the onset of the birth control pill that allowed for more control over pregnancies, and new spousal support laws offering financial security post-divorce, women no longer felt tied to the home. Many were taking full advantage of their newfound freedoms. In 1959, the percentage of married women with small children who worked outside the home was 19 percent. By 1988, it had risen to 58 percent, a trend fueled in part by rising divorce rates, which peaked in 1981, at exactly the time when most Gen Xers were adolescents. The new babysitter? The household's one television. And for many kids, their father figures became Mister Rogers, Dick Van Dyke, and Mr. Brady.

Photo taken by Jill Posner.[4]

While this was a great time to be a woman, it was perhaps less ideal for her offspring. For the first time ever, children found themselves home alone after school for several hours before the rest of the family showed up—thus inspiring the term "latchkey kids." It wasn't until the mid-90s that the public began raising concerns over the potential consequences of leaving millions of children home unattended, and after-school care programs became a standard offering. While research is far from conclusive when it comes to the long-term effects of latchkey childhoods, these children definitely learned at an early age how to take care of themselves (and often, their younger siblings), function independently, and occupy hours of unstructured time.

This is not to say Gen X children were totally ignored by their parents. On the contrary, most middle-class families ate dinner together more often than they do today, parents were actively interested in their children's school performance, and taking an annual family vacation was very much the norm. But when it came to day-to-day routines, parents simply were not encouraged (or pressured) to rearrange their lives around their children. Playgroups and moms' clubs were nonexistent, and it was perfectly acceptable for children in most middle-class neighborhoods to play outside, unsupervised, for hours. What has been referred to as "free-range parenting" today was simply called "parenting" back then. Moms routinely shooed their kids out the door, instructing them not to come back until dinnertime. The "concerted cultivation" style of parenting described by sociologist Annette Lareau—in which parents actively shape and nurture every element of their children's daily lives—did not become the norm for middle-class families until the 1990s.[5]

Whether the hands-off parenting style experienced by the Gen Xers was beneficial or detrimental—or somewhere in between—is a debate for the developmental psychologists. It is, however, often credited as a main factor in the independent, self-motivated work style observed in many Gen X workers. Without the nonstop schedule of supervised, structured activities filling children's daily calendars—what we now consider fairly typical, if not mandatory, for most middle-class American children—Gen X kids had to create their own entertainment, complete their homework without a parent constantly at their side, and make their own "playdates" with the kids in the neighborhood. In other words, Gen X kids had the opportunity to develop the independence, self-reliance, and confidence necessary to get things done in the absence of structure, supervision, or a hand to hold.

Calvin and Hobbes. March 25, 1988[6]

Little Girl in Vintage Room[7]

Chapter 2

Video Killed the Radio Star: from Analog to Digital

"The real problem is not whether machines think but whether men do."

~ B.F. Skinner, *Contingencies of Reinforcement*, 1969

Without question, no other phenomenon has done more to shape the lives of Generation X—along with nearly every other individual on the planet—than the emergence of digital technology.

Generation X is *the* generation that went from analog to digital.

The transition from analog to digital began with the introduction of the home computer and the video game console in the late 1970s, when most Gen Xers were in grade school. By 1984, 16 percent of all households with children under eighteen—i.e., Gen Xers—owned a home computer. By the end of the decade—and with the first Gen Xers entering the workforce—that figure had doubled, and most businesses were already completely dependent on some form of digital technology.

The World Wide Web became publicly accessible in 1991, working its way into mainstream consciousness by 1996, when most Gen Xers were in college, graduate school, or the very early stages of their professional careers. By 1999, almost every country in the world had an Internet connection, with nearly half of Americans reportedly using it on a regular basis, and most businesses scrambling to create an online presence.

Given the timeline of the emergence of digital technology, many would argue Gen Xers were the first leaders of the technological age. Older Gen Xers remember playing Atari Pong as a kid, and younger Gen Xers were "pioneers" on The Oregon Trail. And as adolescents, they were dubbed the MTV Generation. They were, and are, the "bridge generation," with relatively little technology present in their early years, yet nearly ubiquitous by the time they reached adulthood. Compared to Millennials, Gen Xers have had to adapt to a much wider range of technological advances, quite possibly making them the better choice for teaching more "senior" staff how to go digital. Gen Xers are also more cognizant of the presence and impact of technology than their younger counterparts, as well as the pros and cons of society's relatively new dependency on it. Technology may not be as second nature for Gen Xers as it is for Millennials, but certainly Gen Xers are able to function more comfortably with *or* without it compared with the generation that followed them, in both their personal and professional lives.

Sesame Street, Season 7 Cast Photo[8]

Chapter 3

We All Sing the Same Song:
Diversity Makes Its Debut

"Let us love the world to peace."

~ Quoted in *The Angel's Little Instruction Book*
by Eileen Elias Freeman, 1994

Gen Xers enjoy a unique position in pioneering a broader view of diversity. Although they may not have been marching through the streets, fighting for civil rights in the 60s, they have arguably done as much as their parents did when it comes to promoting equality—especially in the workforce.

In 2009, *Sesame Street* turned forty. A hallmark of Generation X, *Sesame Street* was the first television program created with a primary goal of increasing diversity awareness, making Generation X the first cohort of children in American history to grow up hearing the message that ethnic and cultural differences are to be celebrated, not segregated. Before long, major networks began launching sitcoms with unprecedented diversity, as well as unprecedented popularity in mainstream culture: *The Cosby Show, Miami Vice, The Facts of Life,* and *Diff'rent Strokes,* just to name a few.

Gen Xers witnessed and promoted not only an unprecedented increase in issues related to ethnic diversity, but in gender and sexual equality as well. In 1972, Congress enacted Title IX of the Education Amendments, prohibiting sex discrimination in any educational program or activity receiving any type of federal aid.[9] This ultimately led to a sea change in women's athletics—as well as the perception of what girls and women were capable of, both on and off the playing field. And in 1973, the Supreme Court legalized first-trimester abortions, regarded as one of the most significant benchmarks in women's rights.

Prior to the AIDS crisis of the early 1980s, sexual orientation was largely kept out of the public discourse; gay marriage wasn't even on the radar. Then in 1996, NBC launched the first network sitcom to include openly homosexual characters as part of the main storyline—a program targeted specifically at the Gen X demographic, with a cast of Gen X actors, and airing during Gen-X-friendly "Must See TV" Thursdays. The experiment worked: *Will & Grace* ran for eight seasons, and arguably did more for LGBT (Lesbian, Gay, Bisexual, and Transgender) rights than any other public awareness campaign. Gen Xers went from being either silent or negative on the issue of LGBT equality to being the force behind the unprecedented cultural shift in LGBT-related attitudes and beliefs, and the complete turnaround in public policy, including the 2015 Supreme Court decision allowing gay marriage in all states.

It is perhaps not surprising, then, that Gen Xers made up the first truly diverse group of working professionals in our history, and that corporate America finally began to focus in earnest on issues of diversity and inclusion, beginning in the late 80s and early 90s.[10]

From 1987 to 2000, women and minorities made up 64 percent of American college graduates—the first time in our history that white men comprised less than 50 percent of college grads—and 1990 was the first year in which more women earned college degrees than men. The face of the "typical" American white-collar worker was changing, and quickly. Corporate America needed to stop dragging its feet when it came to issues related to diversity and inclusion; Gen Xers were the ones to ignite the fire.

Part II—Generation Xtreme

"Road? Where we're going, we don't need roads."

~ Dr. Emmett Brown, *Back to the Future* (1985)

Debt Problems[11]

Chapter 4

Money for Nothin':
Xers Go into Debt

Economic collapse has punctuated every milestone of our adult lives. When we graduated from high school in the 1980s, Wall Street fell. When we graduated from college, the first Bush recession made jobs impossibly scarce. When we started having children, the Nasdaq crashed. When we finally bought our own homes, the housing bubble burst.

~ Susan Gregory Thomas (Writer, Author, Journalist)[12]

Not to put too fine a point on it, but most Gen Xers are broke, particularly relative to their parents. And it began almost the minute they left home to pursue a college education. During the early 80s, college-aged Americans became prey in many ways to both Sallie Mae (the Student Loan Marketing Association, a publicly traded company that is the largest provider of educational loans in the US) and major credit card companies. Students were told to "take out the maximum" on both counts, which is the opposite of advice given today. Students came to college orientation with credit card companies scrambling to open accounts. Financial Aid counselors on campus actively advised students to take out the maximum amount they qualified for in financial aid each academic year, as it was a "use it or lose it" proposition—if you didn't use it this year, your approved amount would automatically be less the next. And after college?

With more advanced degrees than any previous generation[13], Gen Xers are dealing with an unpleasant side effect from all that education: they hold far more debt than any previous generation, to the tune of about $30,000 on average for those with a college degree or higher.[14] In fact, as of 2013, 54 percent of all outstanding student loan debt was owned by people over thirty-five.

Saddled with student loan debt and just beginning to establish their careers, Gen Xers were hit with the queen mother of all bad omens: 9/11. On September 11, 2001, the median age for Gen Xers was about twenty-eight. In other words, the worst possible time for a disaster to hit as a young adult. They were too old to move back home, (not that that was a popular option for many at the time to begin with), or they were right in the midst of building their careers and families. Not only was this cataclysmic event a blow to the Gen X collective psyche, 9/11 also came with very real economic consequences, exacerbating a recession already underway, with unemployment rates steadily climbing until the spring of 2003.[15]

It was only three years later, just as both the economy and Gen Xers were starting to regain their post-9/11 foothold, that the 2006 housing crisis heralded what was to be the worst economic recession in nearly 100 years. As it turns out, Gen Xers bore the brunt of the 2006 housing crisis and the Great Recession. Between 2007 and 2010, the net worth of people between the ages of 35 and 44 decreased by a whopping 54 percent—far more than any other age group.[16]

With homes underwater, jobs lost, and savings depleted, Gen Xers have had an unexpectedly difficult time building their proverbial nest eggs. According to a Pew Research analysis, "Gen Xers are the least financially secure and the most likely to experience downward mobility in retirement." The bottom line: between student loan debt and lack of savings, Gen Xers are the first generation in history to be less well-off than their parents.

So how does this affect the average Gen Xer when it comes to the workplace? While the exact relationship between debt and career choices remains unclear, there is reason to suspect a link between the two. In a 2011 survey conducted by Pew Research, 24 percent of Americans said student loan debt had influenced their career decisions.[17] According to a recent study by the Federal Reserve Bank of Philadelphia, people with debt (in particular, student loan debt) are less likely to start businesses of their own.[18] Hardly surprising, people with more student loan debt also tend to bypass relatively low-paying public-service jobs for more lucrative fields, like finance and consulting.[19]

Finally, let's not forget the psychological impact of debt. Debt is, by definition, a burden—and not a pleasant one. Also we know (many of us from personal experience) that debt often begets more debt. As previously outlined, many Gen Xers still have years of student loan payments, damaged credit from mortgages they couldn't afford, and huge credit card debt accumulated while trying to keep from defaulting on house payments. It's easy to imagine how a scenario like this could put a real damper on one's outlook on life!

Research supports the link between debt and a whole host of negative side effects. Interestingly, the debt doesn't have to be all that significant to dampen one's outlook on life, either. In fact, a recent Gallup poll found a consistent link between student loan debt *alone* and several areas of well-being. Basically, the more student debt they had, the more likely survey participants were to say they didn't like where they lived, they weren't in great physical health, and they didn't feel like they were getting much closer to achieving their goals. Moreover, it didn't matter if the debt was from 1992 or 2012; the effects on well-being were pretty much the same, regardless of the age of the loan. How much debt are we talking about? For this particular poll, the decline in well-being began at about $25,000 of total student loan debt.[20] If you'll recall, the average student loan balance for Gen Xers is currently around $30,000.

Helicopter Parents[21]

Chapter 5

Family Ties: from Lathchkey Kids to Helicopter Parents

I don't see how this is sustainable. Over forty hours at the office, followed by three hours almost every evening driving my kids from lessons and practices to games and recitals . . . I never get to the gym anymore or even spend time with my husband, let alone my friends! It's too much; at some point, something's gotta give.

~ A Gen X office manager and mother of two

It's a study in extremes: Gen Xers, once referred to as the "neglected generation," have embraced a hands-on model of active parenting unparalleled in our nation's history, keeping their children engaged in a near-constant schedule of activities from the moment they leave the womb until they are shipped off to college. Once the kids enter school age, Gen Xers find themselves coaching sports teams, helping with homework, volunteering at school fairs, and playing taxi driver just about every day of the week.

According to a 2011 report by the Brookings Institute, parents without a high school diploma spent over twice as much time with their kids than their counterparts did in the mid-70s. For parents with a bachelor's degree or higher, the number of hours spent with the kids *quadrupled* during that same period![22]

A similar report by the Pew Research Center showed fathers have nearly tripled the amount of time spent with their kids, as compared to fathers in 1965. And even though the increase for mothers isn't as drastic, they still spend more time with their children today than mothers did at any other time over the last forty years.[23]

Under Pressure[24]

Chapter 6

Under Pressure:
the 24/7 Workday

As the first generation to be defined by e-mail and a globalized workplace, Xers are expected to be connected and available 24/7.

~ Center for Work-Life Policy

Given how much more time parents are spending with their children these days, you might be tempted to assume they are spending less time at the office. After all, there are only so many hours in a day, right?

Turns out, not so much.

With the Internet and cell phones effectively obliterating the boundary between work and home, Gen Xers are the first generation expected to be on the clock around the clock. Gen X workers were the first generation to disrupt their lives with constant work: they get home, feed and bathe the kids, put them to bed, and then jump back online to tackle more work. And this high level of work did not bring with it great rewards. In fact, the opposite was true. Add to that the Great Recession, when companies not only asked employees to take salary reductions—often for the first time ever—but were also laying off record numbers of employees, even though the amount of work remained largely the same.

So what does this look like in real time? In 1975, families earning the median income worked an average of 2,800 hours per year. In 2011, median-income earners were working 3,500 hours per year. In other words, to make roughly the same amount of money in 2011 as your parents did in 1975, you had to work 700 more hours per year (about fourteen hours per week). In two-parent households, primarily the women take on those additional hours. Whereas the number of hours men put in at the office has remained largely unchanged over the past four decades, mothers today spend nearly three times as many hours working outside the home than their mothers—from an average of eight hours per week in 1965 to twenty-one hours per week in 2011.[25]

While most additional hours spent at work are by women, recent years have also seen the emergence of the "extreme job," defined as sixty or more hours per week. Nearly a third of Gen Xers making over $75,000 a year report holding down an extreme job and it's taking a toll on their work-life balance. In a 2007 survey conducted by The Center for Work-Life Policy, nearly 70 percent of "extreme workers" said their jobs undermined their health and well-being. Moreover, almost 60 percent said work got in the way of building strong relationships with their children, and close to half believed it was undermining their marriage.[26]

If statistics aren't your thing, let's boil it down in plain English: Gen Xers spend more time working—both at the office and at home—than any generation before them, without making any more money and while burdened with more debt. In the meantime, they're spending more time with their children than anyone spent with them growing up, while feeling guilty they can't spend more.

"Life moves pretty fast. If you don't stop and look around once in a while, you could miss it."
– Ferris Bueller, *Ferris Bueller's Day Off* (1986)

Part III—Gen X at Work

"And you think what you want about me; I'm not changing. I like . . . I like me. My wife likes me. My customers like me. 'Cause I'm the real article. What you see is what you get."

~ Del Griffith, *Planes, Trains, and Automobiles* (1987)

Chapter 7

Don't You Forget about Me: Gen Xers Feel Passed Over and Pissed Off

"Hello, you've reached the winter of our discontent."

~ Troy Dyer, *Reality Bites* (1994)

Gen Xers have followed a timeline shaped by economic crises and warp-speed advances in technology, all the while scrambling to keep up with unprecedented work-life demands. Now in the prime of their careers, they resiliently soldier the burdens of being the oft-ignored "middle child." Why is this the case? Think about it, dear reader: you even do it yourself. In recent conversations, how often have you said the words "Baby Boomer" or "Millennial" versus the words "Gen Xer"?

During a consulting project, an HR director of a Fortune 500 retail company that underwent layoffs provided this input on the topic of Gen Xers in the workplace. His response was a shocking one.

"Those poor people (Gen Xers) were the ones caught in the cross-hairs during this layoff.

Imagine putting in all those years, doing what you're supposed to be doing and then—BOOM. On the one hand, you can't retire yet, and on the other, you're not a Millennial."

This very bluntly articulates what members of Generation X have been feeling: specifically, that Boomers have kept them from moving upward, and now they are about to be passed over in favor of Millennials. He spoke on condition of anonymity, of course, since his admission—if actually factored into hiring decisions—wanders straight into age-discrimination territory. He also made it clear that while his team focuses on hiring top talent, *they prefer to search within the pool of younger professionals*, in large part because they can be paid less. This is an interesting twist on the generalization that Millennials have a lifestyle that is less expensive to maintain: that they could potentially be "couch-surfing" or living with mom and dad in order to save money. But is there a possibility that this lifestyle could back-fire when it comes to leadership potential in two areas? In how they are perceived regarding leadership attributes (possibly as less self-sufficient and resilient) and/or in how much they are actually offered in pay. While we can hope that this emphasis on youth is not typical of all HR professionals, his quote about Generation X being in the cross-hairs certainly is consistent with what is being heard from actual Gen Xers in the workforce.

> A male business unit leader has seventeen years of seniority with a major manufacturing company and is directly responsible for leading a team bringing in over $200 million in revenue. He says: "I am used to stress, that's part of the job. But above and beyond the stress? Now I have the humiliation of feeling like an idiot. HR and our executive committee are putting time, energy, and money into looking at young people, asking themselves, 'Who do we have here who is high potential (HiPo)? Where are the HiPos?' And here I am with egg on my face. You know what I am? I'm a PoPo—passed over and pissed off."

As a corporate consultant, I have met with countless members of Generation X—ambitious, experienced, career-focused men and women. And what I hear is a resounding theme of discontent, as Gen Xers find themselves bumping up against unexpected ceilings created by Baby Boomers delaying retirement, and ambitious Millennials who have mastered the art of self-promotion. The proverbial middle children of the workforce, many feel ignored and overlooked, stagnating in what they previously assumed would be a mere pit stop on the way to their ultimate destination.

Others are making the same observations. Generational survey research conducted by consulting firms Deloitte and CWLP have turned up similar expressions of discontent among men and women in the middle stages of their careers. A survey by CWLP found that 41 percent of Gen Xers were unsatisfied with the rate at which they were advancing in their organizations, with 49 percent saying they felt "stalled" at work and were fully prepared to leave their current job within the next three years if upward movement remained elusive. The Deloitte survey found that 21 percent of Gen Xers were unhappy with their current positions, and while this number was lower than it was for Millennials, Gen Xers were far more restless, with 58 percent of unhappy Xers actively searching for new jobs, compared to just 32 percent of Millennials.[27]

So why are Gen Xers stuck? They are in the prime of their careers, with a strong portfolio of experience, and a desire to keep moving upward. Why are they feeling ignored, and what's holding them back from reaching their career goals? One fairly straightforward strike against them might be their relatively low numbers. With only 50 million members, Generation X is sandwiched between 78 million Baby Boomers and 80 million

Millennials. These numbers alone might explain how Gen Xers' needs, wants, and demands have been relatively easy to overlook: If you have to make decisions about what is best for your employees, opting for what works best for the most people has some logic to it.

Nevertheless, the comment from the HR director quoted earlier suggests there may be more to Gen X neglect than population. Has a generational "perfect storm" made it uniquely more difficult for Gen Xers to move up the career ladder?

Chapter 8

Back in Time: Out of Sync with Generational Synergy

Gen Xers are a low-slung, straight-line bridge between two noisy behemoths.

~ Pew Research Center[28]

Recently dubbed "America's neglected middle child" by the Pew Research Center, Gen Xers are in many ways the victims of bad timing. Baby Boomers, never particularly interested in the whole aging process to begin with, are holding onto their high-level positions far longer than anyone expected—a stay extended even further after their 401(k)s tanked during the Great Recession. Consequently, many Gen Xers have been waiting patiently for Boomer executives to vacate their corner offices.

Meanwhile, as Gen Xers stagnate in mid-level management, Baby Boomers and Millennials are discovering they have more in common than largesse. Both generations came of age with unfailing confidence in their ability to change the world, taking control of the available public forums to get their message across and their collective demands met—whether for social reform or access to the latest technology in the classroom. As these two generations entered the workforce, they brought that same change-maker energy with them, along with the expectation that their work environments would adjust to suit them, just as every other institution had before.

By contrast, Gen Xers were not raised to view themselves as anything particularly special—hence the "X." They quietly adapted to the work style of Baby Boomers, with the belief that doing so would lead to success and advancement. Instead, Gen Xers may have relegated themselves to "right-hand man" status, coming across as better suited to *support* rather than *lead*, while Millennials impress Boomers with their transformative visions for a better future—and an unfailing belief in their own ability to lead the way.

Baby Boomers also seem to be quite taken with Millennials' effortless mastery of technology, viewing it as the key to remaining competitive. Boomers seem more inclined to perceive Millennials as having the freshest ideas and perspectives, with an instinctive understanding of how quickly one has to shift and adapt to remain ahead of the game in today's ever-shifting markets.

Boomers like to think they see a bit of themselves in these uber-confident upstarts who view age and experience as secondary to energy and passion, much like the Baby Boomers did back when they were known as hippies. As a generation, Boomers have redefined aging because they simply had to. They invented the adage, "Never trust anyone over thirty," and then they inevitably turned thirty and beyond! Boomers still like to credit themselves for everything from the free-love revolution to the invention of sex, drugs, and rock-and-roll—all of which are related to youth and a young lifestyle. There was even a recent article about "Boomsters"[29]—basically, Boomers who are more hip than hipsters. In any case, Baby Boomers have long been enamored with youth, potentially valuing it now more than ever as they stare into the face of their own mortality. Reflecting on their legacy, they may very well regard the vocal, confident Millennials as an ideal choice for carrying their proverbial torches.

This leaves Gen Xers feeling the pressure to prove they, too, are still young enough to be relevant leaders. Think about that for a moment. In the history of corporate America, having to prove one is *young enough* to lead is completely unprecedented! And yet Baby Boomers were the first generation to view youth as an important quality in leadership. The generation before them did not share that belief, but they retired early enough to give Boomers the opportunity to progress virtually unchallenged into senior leadership positions while still in their 30s. Meanwhile, Gen Xers are reluctantly entering their 40s and still waiting for those in charge to retire already, concerned (with good reason) they will have aged into obscurity by the time that moment finally arrives.

I recently interviewed a forty-two-year-old female senior business analyst who did an excellent job capturing a sentiment I've heard many times over:

> "I used to tell myself I was going to stay here as long as possible, do whatever it took to keep working my way up. But the reality? If I stick around much longer, a Millennial will become my boss. They [Millennials] yammer and yammer until they get what they want, and on the other side are a bunch of Baby Boomers hungry and desperate to mentor them in order to feed their own egos and 'leave a legacy.' The synergy of that? I can see the writing on the wall."

Chapter 9

Road to Nowhere: Gen X Neglect— Fact, Fiction, or Product of "Millennial Mystique"?

Never is a long, long word, but it's less frustrating than "God knows when."

~ Mignon McLaughlin, *The Second Neurotic's Notebook,* 1966

Subjective opinions and speculation aside, do we know what is really happening in the hallowed halls of corporate America? To what extent are Gen Xers being recognized for their achievements and moving into leadership positions, as compared to their colleagues both younger and older?

Unfortunately, answers to these questions are elusive. As it turns out, companies are vehemently disinterested in disclosing the ages of the individuals they hire and promote (something about liability), which leaves us with anecdotal perspectives and survey data.

One of the largest recent surveys on the topic, conducted by international consulting giant Deloitte, found that while nearly half (44 percent) of Millennials reported receiving a promotion over the past year, only 21 percent of Gen Xers moved up the corporate ladder.[30] A similar survey, conducted by Canadian firm PwC Saratoga, found similar results: while promotion rates for Millennials remained steady at 20 percent between 2006 and 2010, the rates for Gen Xers actually fell from 11 percent to 10 percent —despite being in their "prime" career years—a result the survey's authors did not expect.[31]

Some of the difference is likely a result of Millennials entering organizations at entry-level positions, thus having more opportunity for advancement. They enter at lower pay-grades, giving corporations more room to promote them without breaking the bank. While no HR leader interested in keeping his or her job will admit to factoring applicants' ages into hiring decisions—let alone publicize data regarding the ages of new hires or promotion recipients—some degree of ageism is virtually inevitable, if for nothing more devious than pure logic.

Recently, a talent management executive (and fellow Gen Xer) at a large, international Fortune 500 company shared his perspective on how age might factor into hiring decisions, specifically when it comes to leadership roles. While he was reluctant to pronounce Gen Xers as being disadvantaged due to specific generational factors—and flat-out dismissed the idea that most companies would favor a less-experienced Millennial over a better-qualified Gen Xer—even he acknowledged that youth has certain advantages; specifically, the number of years a Millennial can potentially give to a company.

> "The reality is, if we're looking at two equally strong candidates, and one is younger than the other, odds are we'll go with the younger one, for the simple reason that they have a longer runway. Even if they don't remain in that specific position, we have more years to move them into various roles within the company as they develop their skill sets. Logically, it's a better investment."

That said, a two-to-one difference in promotion rates is striking, suggesting that a pattern exists that goes beyond the occasional "both candidates being equal" scenario. Gen Xers are bumping up against *two* "gray ceilings": one made up of Boomers disinterested in vacating their leadership positions, while the other—and, arguably, the more insurmountable of the two—is created by Gen Xers' own graying locks.

With Boomers just now starting to phase out of the workforce, Gen Xers (most of whom are in their 40s) have to prove their continued viability as leaders, despite the perception that they have already entered the "waning years" of their careers. With more years of experience often translating to higher salaries, they also have to demonstrate added value. Without the winds of youth at their back, Gen Xers must go the extra mile to show that they, too, not only have fresh ideas and new perspectives just like their younger, hipper, and more energetic counterparts—but also the additional wisdom and experience necessary to translate their ideas into profitable growth strategies for the organization.

During our discussion, this same executive suggested the possibility that some degree of self-fulfilling prophecy might be taking place when it comes to hiring and promoting Millennials over Gen Xers:

> "With all the headlines in the various business journals and online blogs talking about how Millennials are positioned to be the hot new leaders … if hiring decisions really are favoring Millennials, I wonder if it's because we're buying into the hype. In other words, rather than the headlines following actual trends, is it possible that we [i.e., the people who make hiring decisions] are favoring Millennials because we're being told we're favoring Millennials?"

It's a fascinating theory. It seems like every other day we're bombarded with headlines about Millennials-despite their youth and less number of years of experience-being seen as "rock stars" in corporate leadership. I've taken to calling it "The Millennial Mystique." Consider just a few of the headlines I've stumbled across recently:

"Millennials Have Key Business Skills,
Elance-oDesk Survey Finds"[32]

"Millennials Better Poised than Gen X for
Leadership Roles"[33]

"Millennials Will Soon Rule the World: But
How Will They Lead?"[34]

"Why Millennials Could Be the Most
Entrepreneurial Generation Ever"[35]

Now let's look at this theory from the other side. If the hype surrounding Millennials influences hiring decisions, what are the side effects from the many articles and blog posts publicly pronouncing Gen Xers as yesterday's news?

Baby Boomers and the Rising Wave of Millennials Are Hogging the Spotlight, While Gen X Is Struggling[36]

Why Can't Generation X Get Ahead at Work?[37]

Why Gen X Is Unhappy and Hates Working[38]

Are Gen Xers the unpopular, pimply-faced teenagers working at McDonald's because their parents don't have the connections to get them cushy internships downtown?

Again, from the HR executive:

> "Here's the thing: just because Millennials are making a bunch of noise about deserving promotions, have lots of energy and ideas, and may even have an obvious ton of potential, if they don't have the chops, the experience, or whatever, they aren't going to get the job. Which has me wondering if some of these disgruntled Gen Xers are needlessly giving up because of all this talk about how obsolete they are, even if those of us making the hiring decisions aren't necessarily paying much attention to it."

In other words, is it possible that Gen Xers might not be applying for higher-level positions, or asking for promotions, because they've already convinced themselves after reading articles like the ones above that they don't even have a shot? And it is also possible some of the people who make hiring decisions *are* paying attention to Gen Xers' bad press and behaving accordingly?

Chapter 10
The Key Strengths of Gen X Leadership

"Lunch is for wimps."

~ Gordon Gekko, *Wall Street Journal* (1987)

If you have access to mass media of any kind, you have undoubtedly heard and read a lot about the potential benefits of adding Millennials to the workforce. The same media outlets tend to ignore Generation X as much as the typical workplace does. But ignoring the value and potential of Gen Xers at work means companies are actually hurting themselves, because there are many specific leadership benefits Gen Xers bring to the table. So what exactly are the benefits Gen Xers bring? We understand what Gen Xers have experienced as a generation, their work and life from a social psychology perspective; how do those experiences and characteristics translate when it comes to leading?

While of course every individual Gen Xer will have his or

her unique skills, talents, and experiences to bring to an
organization, four primary strengths seem to apply to *many*
professionals from this particular generation: resilience (with
innovative solutions), loyalty (once earned), bridge-building
(middle-child style), and collaboration (with an independent
streak).

RESILIENT INNOVATORS
Gen Xers are highly resilient
change managers, demonstrating
and teaching resilience while
finding innovative solutions
during times of change.

LAST OF THE LOYALISTS
Gen Xers are invested and vested.
Their loyalty is strong once earned,
and keeping them engaged is
the key to holding onto this set
of experienced leaders.

BRIDGE BUILDERS

Gen Xers have witnessed numerous transitions in the business world, and can serve as knowledge and cultural liaisons between Baby Boomers and Millennials.

INDEPENDENT COLLABORATORS

Gen Xers value both collaboration and autonomy, leading teams and projects by facilitating teamwork while encouraging and respecting the value of independent work.

Chapter 11
I Will Survive:
Resilient Innovators

"Try not. Do ... or don't do. There is no try."

~ Yoda, *Star Wars* (1987)

If the idea of a strong leader is someone who can weather a storm, survey the damage, and then quickly figure out how to bounce back stronger than ever, take a much closer look at Gen Xers. Practically bred for change management, most members of Generation X seem almost impervious to having their cheese moved (*Who Moved My Cheese?* Published in 1998) on a regular basis—you might even say they expect it. Few stages of Gen Xers' lives have played out as they were told they would; ergo, they've learned not to *expect* anything.

Further, with neither the predictable career trajectory enjoyed by the Baby Boomers, nor the hand-holding experienced by most Millennials as they prepared for adulthood, Gen Xers often found themselves in unchartered territory with no one around to draw them a map. Most of the unplanned twists and turns Gen Xers have had to navigate came about not as a result of their own actions, but rather the actions of those around them (usually Baby Boomers). Gen Xers have simply borne the brunt of the consequences, and then figured out how to move beyond and rise above them. Achieving their personal and professional goals has required many Gen Xers to discard "the way things have always been done," and instead devise their own unconventional solutions.

Jeremy, a former director-level coaching client, as well as a Gen Xer was placed on a task-force team when his company was thinking of purchasing a new SAP system. This is what his boss had to say after the team completed the job:

> "If we hadn't had Jeremy, we would never have been able to see what was up ahead. I figured the technology part of it would be well received by everyone, because it just made sense. What I *didn't* see was the change management work we had to do to get everyone on board. Jeremy saw it immediately. He knew that we had to talk about the implementation of a new technology-based system differently to different groups, based on where they were with technology. And that we had to really give

it a great deal of thought beforehand, in order for each group to receive it in a positive way."

Despite his boss's rave reviews of Jeremy's work on this and other important projects, Jeremy never received anything more than those kind words: no raise, promotion, or additional opportunities. He was suffering a typical syndrome in corporate America that Gen X experiences: the "Prince Charles" effect, where the Baby Boomers in place had been in place for a long time and were not planning on moving any time soon. Since the typical company follows a pyramid-shaped organizational leadership structure, there are few opportunities to begin with—and Gen Xers have been patiently waiting long past the ages that Baby Boomers were when they took those seats. But Jeremy? He decided he had waited long enough.

Six months later, Jeremy decided to leave the company and move outside of the city to northern Minnesota, where he could spend more time in the great outdoors. He works a flex-time schedule and enjoys his new surroundings.

In reflecting on his experience with his former employer, he acknowledged the frustration he felt in his job, as well as the changes he decided to make as a result: "In the end, not getting what I really wanted at work gave me back what I had somehow lost—my life."

It's disappointing that Jeremy's company failed to retain a truly valuable employee, someone who clearly had the potential to be an excellent leader. Who knows what would have happened had they given him additional opportunities to use his skills, groomed him for future leadership roles—or perhaps simply allowed him more flexibility in his schedule!

Solution: consider involving your Gen X employees in change management efforts, including the opportunity to facilitate conversations and help set the stage for changes to be accepted *before* they are implemented. Consider how you might further leverage these types of skills in other areas of the organization, and be sure to reward their efforts.

Business Dog[39]

Chapter 12
You Really Got Me:
The Last of the Loyalists

"A career? I've thought about this quite a bit, sir, and I would have to say, considering what's waiting out there for me, I don't want to sell anything, buy anything or process anything as a career. I don't want to sell anything bought or processed or buy anything sold or processed or repair anything sold, bought, or processed as a career."

~ Lloyd Dobler, *Say Anything* (1989)

While Gen Xers tend to be regarded as more "independent" than "loyal," I believe this is a misinterpretation of their initial hesitation to buy into things. As a group, the instinctively skeptical Gen Xers are not an easy sell. But once Gen Xers are swayed, they are often highly loyal. Talking about brand loyalty, Linda Gingeri, manager of national advertising for Volvo Cars, spoke in a 2011 interview about winning the loyalty of Generation X—one of their largest target markets—and how the automaker uses transparency and value-oriented campaigns to reach these consumers.

"This consumer group tends to have a relatively high household income so they can afford Volvo cars. However, they examine the products that they buy more from a value and quality standpoint, as opposed to merely following the latest trend. They're not driven by hype or flashiness, and they are skeptical of advertising tactics that are used to manipulate buyer behavior. These consumers can be both cynical and sensible in their purchase behavior, and they are willing to pay a premium for the products that they do perceive as having value."[40]

Translate this over to the world of work, and we are talking about a generation that wants to see who is behind the green curtain before making any major commitments. But once they have vetted their employer, and determined they have a good thing going, they are likely to stay put—well, as long as they feel valued.

If substance isn't a sufficient motivator to stick around, however, straightforward realities could help seal the deal. Many Gen Xers have significant financial obligations, as outlined earlier, thus making risky career moves a nerve-wracking proposition. It's also fair to say that many Gen Xers—given where they are in life—are more likely than their younger counterparts to have roots in their communities, with kids in the middle-school years, and spouses unable or unwilling to relocate. Major life changes, such as a move across the country—or even a cut in pay in exchange for a more satisfying job—are more difficult to fathom when numerous obligations must be considered.

Millennials, on the other hand, tend to have fewer obstacles when it comes to taking risks and moving around, particularly before they've started a family. Millennials are also less likely to place much value on the notion of company loyalty, since the whole "company man" ideal died *long* before they entered the workforce. While Boomers are arguably the most traditionally loyal of the three groups, they are retiring—which leaves Gen Xers as a company's best bet for employees who will stick around when the going gets tough.

Solution: Keep Gen X employees engaged. For this generation, promotions appear to be less important than feeling valued by their employer, and challenged in their role. One option is to establish an Internal Mobility program, allowing Gen Xers (among others) the opportunity to move into different positions within the company. Programs such as these not only keep employees engaged, but they can help strengthen valuable skills while broadening employees' understanding of the organization—and potentially positioning them as perfect candidates for future leadership roles.

Side note: If you have an internal mobility program already—or choose to establish one—make sure your employees know about it. A recent survey by LinkedIn found that while 69 percent of HR professionals reported having an established internal mobility program that "most employees are aware of," only 25 percent of employees reported being aware of an internal mobility program at their organization.[41]

Jump[42]

Chapter 13
Say You, Say Me:
Bridge-Builders and Facilitators

"If you build it, he will come."

~ Field of Dreams (1989)

Members of Generation X and their employers can—and should—leverage Gen Xers' middle-child status, as they are perfectly positioned to serve as the bridge between retiring Boomers and the rising Millennials.

Once Baby Boomers begin leaving en masse, organizations will find themselves in dire need of knowledge transfer. Sandwiched between Boomers and Millennials, Gen Xers have the greatest potential to serve as liaisons, facilitators, and communicators between top executive-level leaders and front-line newbies.

A perfect example of this concept in action took place at an architecture firm in Minneapolis. Many of the employees were Millennials, and they were collectively asking for a more collaborative and creative "we" space. To this end, they convinced two of the firm's partners—along with a director, who happened to be a Gen Xer—to tour a popular collaborative workspace at another organization in downtown Minneapolis. As the group walked around the space, the partners were less than persuaded by the "cool" factor, rolling their eyes and expressing skepticism that beanbag chairs and tents—tents!—had any place in a professional environment, creative or otherwise. As the partners became increasingly dismissive of the whole idea, the Millennials started to get upset, until eventually the Gen Xer sat everyone down and mediated a conversation around what this might look like in *their* office. After the incident, he said, "I was slightly worried it would become a full-blown fight!"

Looking at the chasm that exists between Baby Boomers and Millennials when it comes to business philosophies, work environments, and even communication styles, it becomes painfully clear that a bridge is required if leaders want the company to run at all smoothly in the aftermath of the impending mass retirement of its senior leaders. Gen Xers are not only the obvious choice from a chronological standpoint, they are also at an ideal stage of their careers for this role, having developed their skills under Boomer management, and then later, serving as mentors and managers for Millennials.

Solution: Create roles where Gen Xers are the internal consultants, liaisons, and conduits between the *how* and *why*. They become the liaisons, explaining to younger employees how Baby Boomers originally structured the organization, how change has been managed historically, and how the previous leadership's approach to the business, combined with the fresh ideas and energy brought in by the Millennials, can come together to inform plans for moving forward. Serving in this type of role will also benefit Gen Xers in this phase of their careers, allowing them the opportunity to transfer knowledge while actively demonstrating their ability to build trust and lead Millennials in a collaborative environment.

Emotional Business Meeting[43]

Chapter 14

Hold On Loosely: Independent Collaborators

"I have no formula for winning the race. Everyone runs in her own way, or his own way."

~ Eric Liddell, Chariots of Fire (1976)

Gen Xers are often painted in contradictory terms: fiercely independent and self-sufficient, with a bent toward the cynical, yet somehow equally obsessed with collaboration and arriving at group consensus—sometimes to the point of paralysis. While this could be little more than an example of the problems one faces when trying to paint an entire generation's attributes with a single brush, it is certainly true that members of Generation X do appear to hold a strong "both/and" mentality when it comes to independence versus collaboration in the workplace.

Gen Xers place a high value on the importance of participative decision-making, preferring a relationship-oriented leadership style to the leader-knows-all approach. But they also value their own and others' autonomy and have a high tolerance level for individuation in work style.

As *Fortune* magazine editor Walter Kiechel put it, "As managers, and with remarkable consistency across the group, they espouse values that any progressive organization would endorse: lots of communication, sharing of responsibility, respect for each other's autonomy ... They are also thoroughly uncomfortable with much of what has traditionally... been thought of as the leader's role. They don't like telling others what to do any more than they like being told. [They are] no respecters of hierarchy."

So what do you get when you combine these two traits in a potential leader? Perhaps the perfect person to lead the modern workforce! Companies today are more lateral and team-based than ever. At the same time, over 3.3 million Americans consider home their primary place of work[44]—and millions more work from home a couple days per week. Who better to lead a collaborative team that infrequently occupies the same space than someone who prefers a healthy mix of inclusiveness and independence, who will make the effort to build relationships, ensuring teams are checking in with one another, yet doesn't feel the need to *physically see them every single day* to trust the work is getting done?

In fact, some of the most well-known Gen X leaders also

have been the most public pioneers in the independent-yet-collaborative movement. Yahoo CEO and Gen Xer Marissa Mayer was among the first leaders to publicly declare independence for Yahoo! employees, allowing many of them to telecommute if they so desired. Best Buy pioneered a similar model around the same time, the very popular "ROWE" (Results-Only Work Environment) program, created by two former Best Buy employees, one of whom is—you guessed it—a Gen Xer. Google's Xer CEOs fostered their employees' independent side by implementing their famous "20 percent initiative," giving engineers one day per week to work on pet projects and allowing them to use Google's resources and massive infrastructure to do so.

As you may know, these programs have produced mixed results. And although Mayer ultimately suspended Yahoo's telecommuting program, she did an excellent job capturing the essence of the Gen X independent-collaboration philosophy when explaining her decision: "People are more productive when they're alone, but they're more collaborative and innovative when they're together. Some of the best ideas come from pulling two different ideas together."[45]

Personally, I also wonder if perhaps Mayer and other Gen X leaders tend to overestimate the extent to which Millennials are in touch with their independently productive side. While they may desire a less-structured work environment, Millennials do not necessarily have a lot of experience creating their own structure, something Gen Xers have had to do since childhood. I also think it's important to note that the Gen X leaders listed above quickly adapted their approach when it became clear changes needed to be made (see Chapter 10).

Solution: Allow Gen Xers to take the lead on collaborative projects and teams, placing them in positions where they can create an effective structure that provides for in-person innovation and collaboration, as well as alone time for getting things done. Gen Xers are highly competent team leaders who are self-motivated to set the plan and also empower others to get the work done in their own ways.

Part V—Why Preventing a Gen-Xodus Is Good for Business

"I'm not gonna spend the rest of my life working my ass off and getting nowhere just because I followed rules that I had nothing to do with setting up, okay?"

~ Tess McGill, *Working Girl* (1988)

Chapter 15
If You Leave:
Mind the (talent) Gap!

"It was like coming this close to your dreams and then watch them brush past you like a stranger in a crowd."

~ Dr. Graham, Field of Dreams (1989)

What would happen to your organization if both Baby Boomers *and* Gen Xers vacated their roles around the same time? For a while now, Corporate America has anticipated a "Talent War," with Baby Boomers retiring in droves, leaving Gen Xers and Millennials to duke it out for the corner office. In this scenario, it's easy to imagine how Gen Xers might find themselves being managed by the employees they once mentored. And what if getting passed over in favor of 30-something "high-potentials" (otherwise known as "hi-pos") becomes the proverbial last straw for the more experienced Gen Xers, prompting them to strike out on their own in search of better opportunities…are you and your organization prepared for a "Gen-Xodus"?

If Boomers and Gen Xers leave around the same time, you have a situation on your hands more serious than a Talent War for the best and brightest. From a talent and leadership perspective, we could end up completely skipping the warfare part, and move directly into triage: a talent triage. Allowing a Gen-Xodus to occur within your organization would create an enormous gap in your talent pool. How certain are you that those gaps could be filled any time soon? And at what cost?

Moreover, why would you allow a Gen-Xodus to occur in your organization? They are one of the most highly educated, diverse, and entrepreneurial generations in history. Sure, most of them are in their 40s – an inexplicably invisible decade of life we seem to associate with little more than minivans, mom jeans, and middle management – both in the office and around each abdomen, but still: a lack of "sexy buzz" rarely equals lack of ability.

Perhaps more importantly, your other employees and industry leadership experts also seem to think Gen Xers have what it takes to fill the shoes vacated by retiring Boomers. In 2013, Ernst & Young conducted a survey involving 1,215 full-time professionals – including equal numbers of Millennials, Gen Xers, and Baby Boomers - regarding their perceptions of each generation's managerial skills and general characteristics in the workplace. Consistently, all three generations rated Gen

Xers as the easiest of the three groups to work with in general, and also more likely to possess key leadership skills. Considered far and away the most flexible, communicative, inclusive, and productive, Gen Xers led the pack in their perceived ability to solve problems, develop talent, motivate others, and manage change. Even in the area of technology, Gen Xers fared pretty well: 77% of respondents regarded Gen Xers as tech-savvy, whereas 86% thought the same about Millennials, but only 27% considered Boomers to have much in the way of tech skills.[46]

Chapter 16
Take This Job and Shove It: Gen Xers Are Going Solo

"I am not going to sit on my ass as the events that affect me unfold to determine the course of my life. I'm going to take a stand. I'm going to defend it. Right or wrong, I'm going to defend it."

~ Cameron Frye, *Ferris Bueller's Day Off* (1986)

A Gen X male mid-level manager decided to leave his job and start his own company, saying: "I see articles on LinkedIn about Twenty-Something CEOs. If a twenty-something-year-old can do it, I can take a crack at it. I have savings, and now I finally have my student loans paid off. I'm not going to work in the rat race anymore. After all this time, when I really stop to think about it, I have never received what I need. Heck, I've never even been asked what I need."

This information may sound like "Chicken Little"-style attempt to scare you into promoting your Gen X talent, but this is not a children's story – it is real. Data and anecdotal evidence suggests the sky may indeed be falling. Patient and loyal though they may be, Gen Xers are not going to sit around forever waiting for their moment to shine. They do not hold the "company man" mindset of their parents, and they are tired of stagnating in middle management. As they find themselves near the halfway point in their careers, Gen Xers are starting to think that if they want to reach their ultimate career goals, they may have to take matters into their own hands. They are tired of waiting for the next roles and suffering "The Prince Charles Effect," and on the other side, not all will be highly motivated to train in a younger generation to take their place. Think for a moment: *would you?*

According to a survey conducted by the Center for Work Life Policy (CWLP), 41% of Gen Xers report being unsatisfied with their current rate of advancement. A hefty 49% say they feel "stalled" at work, and about the same number are ready to leave their company in the next three years. Moreover, they don't appear to be bluffing. According to another study – this one by Deloitte – Gen Xers are far more likely to be actively looking for another job than their colleagues. While 38% of Millennials and 37% of Boomers said they would likely remain with their current employer for at least another year, only 28% of Gen Xers expected to stick around, with 22% of them were actively looking for new jobs, compared to just 16% of Millennials.[47]

Chapter 17
Don't You Forget About Me: What's Next

"You see us as you want to see us—in the simplest terms, in the most convenient definitions. But what we found out is that each one of us is a brain...and an athlete...and a basket case... a princess...and a criminal."

~ Brian Johnson, *The Breakfast Club* (1985)

So let's review: Baby Boomers are fixing to retire, en masse. Millennials – while having valuable attributes, including the confidence and even the potential to be great leaders – are today still pretty green around the gills. Meanwhile, you have an entire cohort of seasoned, well-respected, and well-liked Gen Xers, waiting in the wings for their time in the spotlight. But they are tired of being ignored, and getting antsy. If they leave at the same time as your Boomers, you've got yourself a big, gaping hole where talent and experience used to be.

If you are a top leader in your organization who has turned a deaf ear to Gen X for too long, it would be in you and your company's best interest to think about what's next. Perhaps it would be to first re-read Section V, and then take a good, long look at the Gen X leaders in your company. You will probably recognize some of the talents and traits described, and be able to leverage them and actively implement some of the solutions outlined. If you are a top leader who yourself is looking to retire soon, consider transferring some knowledge to and providing some relevant feedback to a Gen Xer. You might be pleasantly surprised at the response and ensuing results.

Lastly, if you are a Gen Xer who picked up this book after reading the title and thinking to yourself, "Hey, that sounds like me!" (or you simply were astonished there WAS a book title with "Gen X" in it!): your next move can be clearly and solidly articulated in this message: now is your time. But you can't sit around quietly waiting for someone to notice. Because the fact is: others noticing Gen X may never happen. In fact, every day there are more and more articles coming out about Generation Z – the ones born after the Millennials. Take a lesson from both the Baby Boomers and the Millennials and speak up. There is a huge leadership development opportunity for Generation X, and that is to better learn how to actively elbow your way up to the front and find your voice. Ensure your organization sees that you have what it takes to lead. Promote the heck out of yourself *before* you get passed over. Because there is no doubt: Gen Xers are ready to lead – and simply need to take the reins.

Chapter 18
Sweet Dreams (Are Made of This): Author's Final Thoughts

"I think we dream so we don't have to be apart so long. If we're in each other'dreams, we can play together all night."

~ Bill Watterson, *Calvin & Hobbes*

As an early member of Gen X (I was born in 1966), my interest in this topic is more than just a professional one. I have lived this story myself, both personally and professionally. I was a kid from Queens, New York, whose parents divorced when I was eight years old. I was a latchkey kid who adored my babysitter (the TV in the living room), and I can spout off 70s TV trivia with the best of 'em. Sesame Street broadcast their first episode on TV when I was three years old, and I watched the very first video on MTV just before starting my sophomore year of high school. In my 20's, I bought into the entire "Yuppie" concept (young upwardly mobile/urban professional) and worked diligently for decades in both my professional and academic careers.

Fast forward to 2015. As a speaker, writer and hospitality experience consultant, I began to hear the same themes with clients over and again. That there are many companies out there fretting about Baby Boomers retiring and scratching their heads desperately trying to attract Millennials. In the meantime, something else was happening behind closed doors: I was hearing poignant and at times shocking stories from the Gen X leaders I was coaching. And these stories were so much more than eye-opening. I felt they were potentially dangerous. Because for years there has been talk of a "talent war" among those in talent leadership. But this faint but growing rumble of discontent meant something more. We were beyond the battles of a war and headed for an all-out Talent Triage.

Then the lightbulb came on when I saw the common threads in these leaders' stories and mine. I had lived this same tale without even realizing it. I myself started my own company in 2013 after working at a company where I felt squelched, under a boss that was younger and less experienced. Ironically, I was at a point in my life when a company could have potentially had my full engagement and loyalty. My kids were about to leave the nest, and I was not at all interested in slowing down. On the contrary: I was finally ready to take my career to the next level. And yet, the distinct vibe I was getting from the organization was that those who were "at the top" were going to steadfastly stay there. Everything seemed to suggest I was never going to be allowed any line of sight to grabbing a brass ring – there were too many others who were holding on tight. So after decades of having worked hard "for the man", I decided it was time to leverage all those years of experience to creating and launching something new.

Leaders – true leaders – understand that success in business requires a keen understanding of people. In response to what I've observed and experienced in Fortune 500 companies and gaping succession holes, I've created a leadership development program specifically targeted to issues related to Generation X. I deliver talks to organizations and at leadership conferences about my generation, and why companies need to do a lot more to leverage the wealth of talent, experience, and strong work ethic we bring to the table. It is my hope that the oft-ignored "middle child" members of Gen X will get a chance to shine, and that my passion for helping every generation work together in mutually beneficial ways is evident on these pages.

"Remember Red, hope is a good thing, maybe the best of things, and no good thing ever dies."

~ Andy Dufresne, *The Shawhank Redemption* (1994)

Mia Mulrennan, Psy.D.

About the Author

Dr. Mia Mulrennan is President and CEO of Rave-Worthy LLC, a consulting and products firm dedicated to helping organizations in customer-centric industries such as travel and hospitality, retail, restaurants and health care. She is a renowned leadership talent and service strategy expert with her doctorate in applied psychology. She is the creator of The Five Factors Survey – a screening survey to find and develop high-touch, customer-oriented talent. She has spent the last twenty-plus years working in Fortune 500 companies and started her career with Marriott and also boutique luxury hotel properties. A thought leader in applying tenets of social, consumer, and organizational psychology to travel and hospitality, she is an adjunct professor at three university graduate business schools including the Masters of Hospitality Management Program at Georgetown University. In her leadership coaching and program work, she has a passion for working with Generation X leaders.

About Terri Bly

Terri Bly is a freelance writer based in St. Paul, MN. She holds a B.A in Theatre and Psychology from Middlebury College, and a PsyD in Clinical Psychology from the Minnesota School of Professional Psychology. She writes for a wide range of professionals and businesses on topics including human resources, psychology, and health and wellness.

Want to Know More?

Rave-Worthy.com
952-451-0017

Dr. Mulrennan has helped organizations leverage the overlooked talents of Generation X and she can help you and your company too.

- Keynote presentations
- Strategy sessions to facilitate implementation of the solutions outlined in this book
- Coaching for Gen X leaders
- Coaching for Leaders wanting to engage their Gen X Talent

Keynote Presentation Descriptions:

The Forgotten Leadership Talents of Generation X
Who They Are, And How They Can Save Your Company

Generation X is known as being the Forgotten Generation. Remember them? They are the generation born between 1965 and 1980 who are sandwiched between the Baby Boomers and Millennials. They are now almost 50, and have leadership talents and strengths that have been overlooked and could very well save your company – and you might not even know it. Learn about these silent an overlooked Xers, and get the scoop on how they just may become the next great leadership heroes of Corporate America.

Talent Triage: Generation X Has Left the Building
Why Gen X Is Not Going To Take It Anymore

From a talent and leadership perspective, there is reason for deep concern regarding an entire generation of leaders. Corporate America has been deaf to Gen X for too long. What would happen to *your* organization if both the Baby Boomers and Gen Xers started to leave at around the same time? For many years now, a "Talent War" has been anticipated, with the Baby Boomer's looming retirement on the horizon. But having Boomers and Gen Xers leave around the same time is more serious than a Talent War for the best and brightest. From a talent and leadership perspective, we might end up completely skipping the warfare part - and move directly into triage - desperately trying to compress hemorrhaging that might never be stopped. Don't let this happen to your company.

References and Citations

[1] 1985. *The Breakfast Club*. (Photograph). Used with permission, Universal Studios.

[2] Ferro, R. (Photographer, St. Petersburg Times). 1969. *Lady, is this your litter?* (Photograph). Used with permission, The Tampa Bay Times, originally licensed by Life magazine for their May 30, 1969 issue.

[3] Thomas, S. (2010). *A Teacher's Guide to Generation X Parents.* Retrieved from www.edutopia.org/generation-x-parents-relationships-guide

[4] Posner, J. (Photographer). [Fiat billboard with graffiti]. (Photograph).

[5] Lareau, A. (2011). *Questions and Answers: Unequal Childhoods: Class, Race, and Family Life.* Retrieved from sociology.sas. upenn.edu/ sites/sociologysas.upenn.edu/files/ Lareau_Question&Answers.pdf

[6] Watterson, B. (Writer). 1988. *Calvin and Hobbes.* (Comic strip). Used with permission, Universal UClick.com

[7] Lunamarina. (Photographer). 2011. *Camera Retro Photo Little Girl in Vintage Room.* (Photograph). Used with permission, iStockphoto.com

[8] 1975. *Season 7 Cast Photo.* (Photograph). Used with permission, Sesame Workshop.

[9] Women's Sports Foundation. (2011). *Title IX Legislative Chronology.* Retrieved from www.womenssportsfoundation.org/ home/advocate /title-ix-and-issues/history-of-title-ix/history-of-title-ix

[10] Anand, R. and Winters, M. (2008). *A Retrospective View of Corporate Diversity Training from 1964 to the Present.* Retrieved from www.wintersgroup.com/corporate-diversity-training-1964-to-present.pdf

[11] Lightsource. (Graphic Designer). *Debt Problems*. (Graphic). Used with permission, Depositphotos.com

[12] Thomas, S. (2010). *A Teacher's Guide to Generation X Parents*. Retrieved from www.edutopia.org/generation-x-parents-relationships-guide

[13] Miller, J. (2013). *Lifelong Learning: Generation X Illustrates the New Reality*. Retrieved from www.lsay.org/GenX_Vol2Iss3.pdf

[14] Smialek, J. (2014). *College Debt Leaves Generation X Grads Less Wealthy than Parents*. Retrieved from www.bloomberg.com /news/2014-09-18/college-debt-leaves-generation-x-grads-less-wealthy-than-parents.html

[15] Amadeo, K. (2015). *How the 9/11 Attacks Still Affect the Economy Today*. Retrieved from useconomy.about.com/od/Financial-Crisis/f/911-Attacks-Economic-Impact.htm

[16] Smialek, J. (2014). *Lean Retirement Faces U.S. Generation X as Wealth Trails*. Retrieved from www.bloomberg.com/news/articles/2014-06-09/lean-retirement-faces-u-s-generation-x-as-wealth-trails

[17] Pew Research Center. (2012). *College Graduation: Weighing the Cost… and the Payoff*. Retrieved from www.pewresearch.org/2012/05/17/college-graduation-weighing-the-cost-and-the-payoff/

[18] Korkki, P. (2014). *The Ripple Effects of Rising Student Debt*. Retrieved from www.nytimes.com/2014/05/25/business/the-ripple-effects-of-rising-student-debt.html

[19] Korkki, P. (2014). *The Ripple Effects of Rising Student Debt*. Retrieved from www.nytimes.com/2014/05/25/business/the-ripple-effects-of-rising-student-debt.html

[20] Gallop Purdue Index Report. (2014). *Great Jobs Great Lives*. Retrieved from www.wsac.wa.gov/sites/default/files/2014.ptw.(60).pdf

[21] Sangoiri. (Graphic Designer). *Helicopter Parents*. (Graphic). Used with permission, Depositphotos.com

[22] Sawhill, I., Reeves, R., and Howard, K. (2013). *Parenting, Politics, and Social Mobility*. Retrieved from www.brookings. edu/research/articles/2013/09/09-parenting-gap-social-mobility-reeves-sawhill

[23] Parker, K., and Wang, W. (2013). *How Mothers and Fathers Spend Their Time*. Retrieved from www.pewsocialtrends.org/2013/03/14/chapter-4-how-mothers-and-fathers-spend-their-time/

[24] Alphaspirit. (Photographer). *Under Pressure*. (Photograph). Used with permission, Depositphotos.com

[25] Greenstone, M., and Looney, A. The Hamilton Project. (2011). *The Great Recession May be Over, But American Families are Working Harder than Ever*. Retrieved from www.brookings.edu/blogs/jobs/posts/2011/07/08-jobs-greenstone-looney

[26] Hewlett, S., Luce, C., Southwell, S., and Bernstein, L. (2007). *Seduction and Risk: The Emergence of Extreme Jobs*. Center for Work Life Policy Report. Retrieved from Center for Talent Innovation, www.talentinnovation.org/publication.cfm?publication=1060

[27] Kwan, A., Neveras, N., Schwartz, J., Pelster, B., Erickson, R., and Szpaichler, S. (2012). *Talent 2020: Surveying the talent paradox from the employee perspective*. Retrieved from www.deloitte.com/assets/dcomglobal/local%20assets/documents/human%20capital/us_talent2020_september2012_09142012.pdf

[28] Taylor, P., and Gao, G. (2014). *Generation X: America's neglected 'middle child'.* Retrieved from www.pewresearch.org/fact-tank/2014/06/05/generation-x-americas-neglected-middle-child/

[29] Lear, K. (2015). *Boomster: The Baby Boomer Hipster.* Retrieved from Bridgeworks, thegenerationspeople.wordpress.com/2015/03/16/boomster-the-baby-boomer-hipster/

[30] Kwan, A., Neveras, N., Schwartz, J., Pelster, B., Erickson, R., and Szpaichler, S. (2012). *Talent 2020: Surveying the talent paradox from the employee perspective.* Retrieved from www.deloitte.com/assets/dcomglobal/local%20assets/documents/human%20capital/us_talent2020_september2012_09142012.pdf

[31] PriceWaterhouseCoopers LLP., Saratoga, Ontario, CA. (2012). *Value through your people: Workforce performance in Canadian banking.* Retrieved from www.pwc.com/en_CA/ca/people-change/publications/pwc-workforce-performance-canadian-banking-2012-02-en.pdf

[32] Staffing Industry Analysts. (2014). *Millennials have key business skills, Elance-Odesk survey finds.* Retrieved from www.staffingindustry.com/Research-Publications/Daily-News/Millennials-have-key-business-skills-Elance-oDesk-survey-finds-31989#sthash.hp8DEHTU.dpuf

[33] The Globe and Mail, in consultation with Thomson Reuters. (2015). *Millennials better poised than Gen X for leadership roles.* Retrieved from www.theglobeandmail.com/partners/thomsonreuterscapitalize/millennials-better-poised-than-gen-x-for-leadership-roles/article21575563/

[34] Bersin, J. (2013). *Millennials Will Soon Rule the World, But How Will They Lead?* Retrieved from www.forbes.com/sites/joshbersin/2013/09/12/millennials-will-soon-rule-the-world-but-how-will-they-lead/

[35] O'Brien, J. (2014). *Why Millennials Could be the Most Entrepreneurial Generation Ever.* Retrieved from www.americanexpress.com/us/small-business/openforum/articles/why-millennials-could-be-the-most-entrepreneurial-generation-ever/

[36] Crosby, J. (2014). *Baby boomers and the rising wave of Millennials are hogging the spotlight, while Gen X is struggling.* Retrieved from m.startribune.com/lifestyle/relationship/283229861.html

[37] Alsop, R. (2013). *Why can't Generation X get ahead at work?* Retrieved from www.bbc.com/capital/story/20130710-the-forgotten-generation

[38] Donohue, M. (2014). *Why Gen X is Unhappy and Hates Working.* Retrieved from www.huffingtonpost.ca/mary-donohue/millennials-_b_5239628.html

[39] Willeecole. (Photographer). *Business Dog.* (Photograph). Used with permission, Depositphotos.com

[40] Lawson, M. (2013). *Customer Loyalty: What do You Know About Generation X?* Retrieved from epmsonline.com/customer-loyalty/customer-loyalty-what-do-you-know-about-generation-x

[41] Linkedin Talent Solutions. (2013). *2013 Global Recruiting Trends Top Five Talent Acquisition Trends You Need to Know Now.* Retrieved from business.linkedin.com/content/dam/business/talent-solutions/global/en_US/site/pdf/datasheets/linkedin-us-recruiting-trends-2013-en-us.pdf

[42] Olly18. (Photographer). *Jump.* (Photograph). Used with permission, Depositphotos.com

[43] DragonImages. (Photographer). *Emotional Business Meeting.* (Photograph). Used with permission, Depositphotos.com

[44] Lister, K. Global Workplace Analytics. (2013). *Latest Telecommuting Statistics*. Retrieved from globalworkplaceanalytics.com/telecommuting-statistics

[45] Tkaczyk, C. (2013). *Marissa Mayer breaks her silence on Yahoo's telecommuting policy*. Retrieved from fortune.com/2013/04/19/marissa-mayer-breaks-her-silence-on-yahoos-telecommuting-policy/

[46] Ernst & Young LLP. (2013). *Younger managers rise in the ranks: survey quantifies management shift and reveals challenges, preferred workplace perks, and perceived generational strengths and weaknesses*. Retrieved from http://www.ey.com/Publication/vwLUAssets/EY-Survey_shows_younger_managers_rising_in_the_ranks/$FILE/Executive-Summary-Generations-Research.pdf

[47] Kwan, A., Schwartz, J., and Liakopoulos, A. (2011). *Talent Edge 2020: Building the recovery together*. Retrieved from dupress.com/articles/talent-edge-2020-building-the-recovery-together

Printed in Great Britain
by Amazon

18171881R00078